PUSHKIN PRESS

# Salad Anniversary

"A potent, distilled brew, like the headiest saké"

*The Lady*

"*Salad Anniversary* is an acutely self-aware portrait of modern life and love... It is no wonder this book triggered a cultural phenomenon in Japan. She describes the source of her desires and frustrations with such precision that they become universal"

*Asymptote Journal*

"Tawara is a champion of gratitude and glee... her verses are full of zest... a fruitful collection"

*New Orleans Review*

"These poems are alive, fizzing with vitality, dripping with honesty. It is little wonder the original publication was such a phenomenon"

*Japan Times*

"Fresh, light, wonderful"

*Le Point*

T0286556

MACHI TAWARA (b. Osaka, 1962) is one of Japan's most popular tanka poets and is credited for giving new relevance to this millennia-old Japanese poetic form. Her first volume of tanka, *Salad Anniversary* (1987), became an immediate bestseller and turned its author into an instant celebrity. *Salad Anniversary* inspired televised serial dramas, a musical revue and a full-length movie, and went on to sell 8 million copies worldwide. She has been awarded multiple prizes for her poetry, including the Kadokawa Tanka Award and the Modern Japanese Poets Association Award. Tawara is also a critic, translator and travel writer, and contributes to various national newspapers and magazines in Japan.

# SALAD
# ANNIVERSARY

MACHI TAWARA

# SALAD
# ANNIVERSARY

Translated from the Japanese
by Juliet Winters Carpenter

PUSHKIN PRESS
LONDON

Pushkin Press
Somerset House, Strand
London WC2R 1LA

*Sarada Kinenbi* by Machi Tawara
Original text © 1987 Machi Tawara
English translation © 1989 Juliet Winters Carpenter. All rights reserved.

Originally published in Japanese by
Kawade Shobo Shinsha Ltd. Publishers, Tokyo

English translation originally published by
Kodansha International, Ltd., Tokyo

English translation and publication rights arranged with Kawade Shobo
Shinsha Ltd. Publishers through The Staley Agency, LLC, Tokyo

First published by Pushkin Press in 2014
This edition first published in 2018

5 7 9 8 6 4

ISBN-13: 978-1-78227-457-5

Designed and typeset by Tetragon, London
Printed and bound by Clays Ltd, Elcograf S.p.A.

www.pushkinpress.com

# Contents

## August Morning

Always playing this song
you race along the seacoast road—
"Hotel California"


I watch you on your surfboard
poised between blueness
of sky and sea


Beach picnic for two—
thinking of egg sandwiches
never even touched

Sitting against a sunny wall—
your legs and mine,
parallel lines


On Kujukuri Beach
taking picture after picture
I may only throw away


Is there anything more?
More to believe, more to want?
Sprawled side by side on sand


Fat oval sun
can't bear the burden
of its own weight

Under an orange sky on Kujukuri Beach
I snuggle up to you
in monochrome


The gentleness of lapping waves
makes me unafraid
to hear you say good-bye


You and I on the night beach
face to face in silence—
a sparkler softly sputters


Enjoying your hesitation,
I watch you hunt for words
to break the silence

Your left hand,
exploring my fingers one by one—
maybe this is love


This too a memory,
I leave it as it is—
dent in my straw hat


"Call again," you say, and hang up—
I want to call again
right now


"Sorry," I say lightly
as if to a friend—
Father just stares into his teacup

In the fitting room
I suddenly find my arms full
of floral prints you like


So huge
it gladdens my heart—
this store's shopping bag


Happiness of standing before a grocer's
at four in the afternoon
planning the supper menu


After you have gone
evening gathers in my heart—
all the scenery is you

Another Saturday of waiting for you.
Time spent waiting—
food a woman lives on


In the ballpark,
midday made before our eyes,
we shine


My team in a tight spot—
I look on somehow happy,
leaning against you


Your hand
signaling for a draft beer
catches my eye and absorbs me

On my birthday
a year seems short,
a day long


The rose blooms,
pretending not to know
that 400 yen made it mine


"Call me again" "Wait for me"
Your love is always spoken
in commands


Glancing up at the falling rain
suddenly I want
your lips

Escape from a shower into a street stall
and drink a glass of cheap saké—
fun to be alive


The woman in the street stall
calls me your wife—
and so, for a while, I am


At a tiny shop
like a child's play store
I buy you a toothbrush


Warm—knowing
when I say "I'm cold,"
you're there to say "Me too"

With the man I want to spend my life loving
my heart aches—
thinking of the slender margin
    between unreal and real


"Today only!"
Red blouse in the window,
on sale each time I go by


You love boiled tofu for dinner.
Remembering,
I buy a little earthen pot


Cosmos flowers sway
in front of model homes
no one will ever live in

Pick up the receiver,
happy someone thought of me
in the middle of the night


Wednesday your words "See you"—
the same as ever
yet somehow not


On Thursday, wanting despite myself
to trust you,
I wear a psychedelic T-shirt


Unanswered ring tells me you're still out
Where have you gone drinking?
Who's getting drunk with you?

Thinking you too must be
listening to this radio show
I switch it off in mid-laugh


"It's okay with me," you say—
not understanding what's okay,
I nod


I can't believe you mean
all that counts is a good time—
do I know you?


Late afternoon—
you and I gaze at the same thing
as between us something ends

Sitting in a coffee shop
with a man who isn't you,
making him say, "Then I'll wait five years"


Lights at dusk
in Heartbreak Hotel—
a place you sang of once


Remember the August morning
you started up the engine
and carried me away?


Like getting up to leave
    a hamburger place—
that's how I'll leave
that man

Like a whiskey bottle on reserve too long
that man's no longer mine—
skies are clear today


It's enough to be your lover
sings someone in a song,
making it sound so easy


Now that I wait for you no more,
sunny Saturdays and rainy Tuesdays
are all the same to me

# Baseball Game

Wrapped in a green sweater
as though folded deep in your arms—
winter comes on


On a Sunday morning
fragrant with navel oranges,
I boil two eggs to perfection


I check my tear-stained reflection,
remembering that you said
"Stay beautiful"

More than dozens of words of love,
one chill word
preoccupies me


Knight in leather jacket
astride your motorcycle,
for you let the sunset blaze!


Underline the words
hard enough to tear the page—
"to love and not have faith"


Eating takeout sushi with you,
only 300 yen—
tastes so good I know I'm in love

Shielded by you in a crowded train,
I gaze up close
at fine down on your face


Every time I look at the public bath wall,
three of them lined up for sale—
"ear-cleaning sets"


With you, for better or worse,
even when I'm gargling
I feel like a woman


Longing to see
the ocean in December,
we board the Romance Express

A day playing at Enoshima Beach—
you have your future, I mine,
and so we take no snapshots


Grieve with me—
the sureness of your touch
    catching Frisbees
is missing in this romance


Throwing stones in the waves,
he never looks my way—
young man wild like the sea


I cherish the bit of crimson
staining your finger
as you open a raw oyster for me

Skeptical of promises,
you don't even bother
to build your castle away from the waves


"Machi-chan"—
I like the moment he hesitates
before using my pet name


The smell of you dances on the salt breeze
and in your arms
I turn into a seashell


"Marry me,"
after two canned cocktails—
are you sure you want to say that?

Head cradled in my lap like a child,
lonely vagabond
you breathe quietly, asleep


Five-thirty p.m.—
you and I walk on sand, kissing
under the eye of Mt. Fuji


— "I was born to run," you say—
for you who have no hometown
I want to become the sea


"I'm going to go feel the winter waves,"
I say, and walk away—
unable to meet your gaze on the beach

Unable to accept this love—
walking back at the hour
when big hand and small hand overlap


Don't forget
the broken wing of the airplane
we buried together in sand


Loneliness drifts down in December—
in my life, one plus one
forever makes two


Ancient love poems
touch my heart this evening—
to each one I give a star

Using your hairbrush
to brush my hair
I savor your male smell


A morning of waiting for you—
at four, at five-thirty, again at six,
I check the alarm clock dial


"Till I'm thirty
I'll stroll through life," you say—
what scenery am I to you, I wonder?


Evening, and I wonder—
how long was her hair?
the girl who lived in this room with you

Aren't you cold?
Alone, hanging in midair,
you float through life unattached


River of taxis
at two a.m.—
crosswalk fast asleep


"Today the public bath was closed."
I want to spend every day
talking of little things like that


Knowing the smallness
of a man who thinks only of me,
I still can't help wishing you would

"Today makes exactly 500 days
since we met," he whispers—
surprised, I jump away


Like snow drifting down
from where my mother lives—
loneliness in Tokyo


February begins—
for the next two months,
everything a memory


For some reason
it is woman's lot to know
people cannot live on love

In Yokohama's Chinatown
perhaps for the last time—
buying a smile-shaped cookie


Cooking an omelet
flavored with tears
of coming morning and farewell


Valentine's Day away from you—
I spend the day
like the priestess of a shrine


Realizing that was the night
of our first kiss,
I shut my diary with a bang

You hold me tight,
as if I were going far away—
March, the month of good-bye


In March, my heart indifferent
to the coming spring,
I gaze with you at late plum blossoms


Unable to say what waits to be said
this early afternoon,
we focus on the baseball game


Two outs, bases loaded—
you crouch, tense, as if it were
a major life crisis

Passing each other on escalators
headed in opposite ways—
happy to be with you if only for a moment


Around the unbending telephone pole,
no blossoms to scatter or bud,
spring breezes play


As a monument to my youth
I hang at my window
a plant called "bridal veil"

# Morning Necktie

Set off to see for myself
my father's name
carved in a Tohoku museum


Once the "world's strongest,"
my father's magnet
crouches on a shelf


Monday morning
the head of the Magnetic Research Institute
picks out his necktie

My father, perfectly at home
with rare earth elements,
loves Modigliani women


"Writing more love poems?"
half humorously
half anxiously


His present—
Sanuki noodles—
comes stuffed in a company envelope


Something warm in the way
he calls his wife "Mother"
without the least hesitation

He wipes his face with a hot towel
and sighs contentedly—
looking at him now I see an ordinary man


Moving away from the telephone
he sips his tea as if to say
"I'm not listening"


Forgiven
their inability to express tenderness—
men of my father's generation

# I Am the Wind

A letter overflowing with love
love that belongs
to the date on the postmark


I finish writing, put on the stamp,
and time begins to flow
toward the moment of your answer


Signaling the start of my vigil,
it stands sharply at attention—
corner mailbox

You have your Saturdays, I know—
mine are spent
pretending not to notice


Turn down my fourth invitation.
Sundays I do nothing—
this day belongs to me


Beneath your hard-bitten ways
I see a boy—
his skies are wide and blue


Floating together down the spring street—
this afternoon I want
to be seen by everyone

I don't leap before I look—
look for what, anyway?
just slide along in life


Eyes shut, face buried in your beer mug,
you don't even look at me—
what is it that you thirst for?


Two more hours
and I turn into Cinderella—
you go on about nuclear war


After this nuclear war you speak of,
turn with me, in the ruins,
into a flowing stream

"You have a bone to pick with me,
    don't you?"
arbitrarily you say—
maybe I do, at that


A break in the rainy season—
the ragman making his rounds.
Won't you trade my memories for
    a pack of pocket tissue?


Thursday afternoon
I twirl the dial,
just to make a noise in your room


"I'll die at thirty," you say,
and I in turn decide
not to die till then

Eighty kilometers an hour—
clinging to your back, I am the wind—
now there is only my arms around you


On her neckline the trace
of last year's bathing suit,
she hears the ocean call


Told "I want you, Machi-chan"
my heart wants to follow him—
like children playing a game


Only eighty years to live—
yet the "whys" of twenty-one
resist everything

This 365-faced polyhedron, my self—
let it flee flow fly apart,
take off!


"When you get around to it."
Knowing you will never call
I take revenge in a sugary voice


Rise, pale sun—
this autumn premonition
of losing you


There is one who loves me
randomly—a "me"
that isn't me at all

If no one wants you
by the time you're twenty-nine
give me a call, I made him say


Like someone from another planet—
but not really—
a friend whose surname changed
    from Maeda to Ishii


Ill effects of low blood pressure—
no more worrisome
than my daily horoscope


At the end of day they lie on my finger,
slightly clouded—
contact lenses

Really, you see everything
don't you now,
I whisper to the small, round lenses


Scrub my contact lenses hard
as if washing off the soil
of what they've seen


Bought a chatty birthday card—
a swarm of words
to cover the blank in me


What are you doing,
    what are you thinking?
A romance made up of questions
is only a lifeless shell

Junk mail it may be
but still this postcard cheers me—
autumn evening


Waiting for your call—
wondering just how drunk you were
when you said those things to me


Ring after ring tells me you're out—
I listen fondly,
grateful for any clue


Spaces in my appointment book
I'd been saving for you—
I fill them in, in pencil

Unable to make even one love mine,
I chew idly
on overcooked cauliflower


At my side
you liken our relationship
to me and my potted parsley


In Yokohama,
atop Harbor-Viewing Hill,
we probably look like lovers


Like lingering to watch a street pantomime
and gazing for a moment
into the performer's eyes

Van Gogh exhibit—
move from one painting to the next,
seeing in the glass just my own face


Your memory of that day—
a day you say changed your life—
has nothing to do with me


Evening, and I wish
you and I were anatomical models
labeled simply "human"


"I want to eat, and not gain weight!"
So goes the commercial.
I want to be loved—
    and not to have to love

I turn up the volume all the way,
listening to the Southern All Stars—
all around, everything is weeping

# Summertime Ship

Slowly, like the earth waking,
it starts to move—
summertime ship


Amid torn paper streamers
in the summer wind
I sail for Shanghai aboard the *Jianzhen*


On the dark blue surface
of the East China Sea—
only sky, only waves

"All the lies you ever told
don't really mean a thing,"
the ocean seems to say


Each one on deck with a private breeze,
a private time when conversation
isn't wanted


Suddenly wonderful—
that each tiny islet from my porthole
should have a name


Beer on the table tilts in the glass—
that's right, I'd been forgetting:
East China Sea

Bearing a wind that calls me inland,
color of milk caramel—
Yangtse River


A little Chinese girl
dances in court costume
like a windless summer day


"Detour!"
Lively, glittering Shanghai streets,
crammed with bicycles and men at work


Bottles of Tsing Tao beer cry out
as the truck zooms round the corner—
Shanghai

Must be getting fond of this place—
my second washday
in Xi'an


Seven days since I left home—
suddenly I wonder,
who's in first in the Central League?


Stare at foxtails swaying in Xi'an
just as they do
in paddies back home


This path sprinkled with
yellow sunflowers
stretches on to the Silk Road

Hundreds upon hundreds of figures
in the terracotta army—
their thoughts sleep standing


Looking at the residence of Yang Guei-fei,
wish I had a man
who'd dig a pond for me


Ripples on its surface
like babies' sighs—
Yellow River in midsummer


After three days watching Mr. and
    Mrs. Po,
at last I see
husband and wife are only lovers

As I walk alongside Mr. Po,
faint stirrings of jealousy
in Mrs. Po


Wind on the summit of Qianling—
I gaze down on an endless
mosaic of fields


In Xi'an—
city where all fruit is sour—
the morning breeze is born


Big Wild Goose Pagoda,
standing with the new-risen sun—
farewell, Xi'an

My eyes grow tired
in fields so vast
they laugh at all my words


Passport in tow, Machi Tawara—
whether she is here or not
North China plain goes on


Daubed with sunscreen,
my face shines the color of rice grains
in Luoyang


"Two for one yen!"
Little Chinese girls hawking souvenirs
cluster like thunderclouds

Though in Japan I never wanted them,
here I buy scroll paintings,
here I buy stone rubbings


In Luoyang, waiting for a bus
in the shadow of a tree—
I came here once before I was born


In Luoyang
the youth selling "banana apples"
has such long legs


The train plies the continent
westward, westward—
I close my eyes, wanting the sea

In a sleeping berth
that oozes earth-colored sweat
I hear a whistle scream


Drone of cicadas in a bamboo grove,
like a dizziness—
listening, I become bamboo


Handkerchief spread on my lap,
square and hot—
Hangzhou, city of body heat


Looking afar at Qiantang Bridge,
I watch a green train
snip off the wind

Before I know it
they're calling me "Mat-chan"—
Wang and Little Chiang


Set off through Tokyo streets
wearing the T-shirt I wore
when I saw the Yangtse

# Wake-up Call

It starts before
my wake-up call to you—
in Etiquette Lion toothpaste foam


Rattling me along
to where you wait in Shinjuku—
the Odakyu Line is my Silk Road


Sweet-sour cherries
  on the rooftop terrace—
right now I feel
more loved than anyone

He loves the way
I look at my watch—
quiet fills my heart


Secretly I try on your jacket,
drinking in your smell,
and strike a pose like James Dean


"Life should be dramatic!" you declare—
for me a dramatic
supporting role


Morning—I sip milk,
listening to the song "Downtown Boy,"
missing you

Remembering your joke,
I giggle out loud
in the middle of a crowd


My heart racing at the color of the sea—
a color I had never known—
I scribble in my notebook
    "Kujukuri Beach"


Beautiful—
in the park, close to twilight,
the gait of a pregnant woman


If tomorrow is never going to come
I'll tell you everything
before I go to sleep

What bird is that?
May morning, you wake up crowing
"Terr-ific!" "Terr-ific!"


May of my twenty-first year—
the word "motherhood"
a pure abstraction


Like 100% juice
from finest Valencia oranges,
unstrained


Sunday morning—
in sandals, we set off together
to shop for bread and beer

The number 12 is sweet—
I live to hear your voice
at midnight


Arriving at the station one minute early,
I spend one minute
thinking of you


Every morning, a sense of repose
after passing a storefront
lined with fragrant buns


Moon of the sixteenth night—
whatever thread that bound us,
snapped

Is there no new love?
Not really seeking,
I mutter to myself at dusk


"Woman in a Blue Hat,"
    that painting I saw with you—
even now she droops her head
in the Sculpture-Forest Museum


After a week of not seeing you,
now, like radish cooked too long,
the flavor is too strong


At the beach stall,
    sipping a glass of cheap saké,
the old woman's words of wisdom
burn in my stomach

Watching together a love scene
In close-up on TV—
the actor's movements so like you


Carrying French bread
after the wake-up call,
I mount the stairs two at a time


Writing left-handed,
    your gestures are blue—
taking off your glasses,
warm yellowish-green


He loves me, he loves me not;
if only I had as many loves
as petals

Warm fall day—
down Waseda Avenue trudges
    a band of musical sandwichmen,
hoping no one will look

# Hashimoto High School

Kanagawa Prefectural Hashimoto
    High School—
here the kids call
Machi-chan "teacher"

All making the most of this
    classroom hour,
each in our own way—
ninety-two eyeballs, and me

Daigo, Katsuji, Ken'ichi, Shumei—
I read in each name
the pride of the christener

Girls in middy blouses
scurry through the streets
as if keeping someone waiting


Writing the characters for "youth"
somehow I'm struck
by all those horizontal lines


Now that I've learned their names
each pupil's answer sheet
takes on a personality


Writing on the blackboard,
    I pause to rest my hand—
in those seconds
think meltingly of you

Standing before the class—
my hairdo, my waistline too,
the focus of attention


Toss my attendance book
and navy blazer in the air—
on weekends I'll be sweet and feminine


Commuter train shakes
with the cruelty of junior high girls
passing judgment on their teachers


As I grind the ink,
thoughts come rising to the surface—
grind all the harder,
    as if to strike them down

Midsummer day in a classroom corner—
writing out characters
for "snow" and "fire"


My heart returns stubbornly
to a certain point—
ink isn't black enough to blot out memory


This June, full of memories
I'd rather forget—
I set down the glass paperweight


Rinsing my brush at the sink,
the irregularity of the flow
fascinates me

Your teenage years—
slightly twisted by the song
"A Boy on the Backstreet"


Take my place at the podium
after boning up for twenty minutes
on a poet who died young


Chinese compound meaning
     "wasted effort"—
made up of characters for "pupil"
and "hard labor"


Night of August 31,
tail end of summer vacation—
writing my mother a long long letter

New eraser for eighty yen,
new band on my wristwatch—
second term begins


In the corridor, our greetings
a bit self-conscious—
first day of the new term


"Oh yeah?!" the new catch phrase—
in the classroom, student conversations
get by on just "Oh yeah?" "Oh yeah!"


At the window, proctoring an exam—
all is cheerless save
a supermarket sign

Smelling faintly of shampoo,
the kids solve problems
in differential and integral calculus


Proctoring the exam,
suddenly I think of each one's mother
the day she conceived this child


Parents claim to raise their children,
but garden tomatoes turn red
unbidden


As I proctor the math exam,
one girl keeps watching
my every move

# Pretending to Wait for Someone

Wanting to be Tinkerbell
and take you in my arms—
pearly pink flat shoes


After seeing you off this morning,
I glance at my toothpaste tube—
the dent in it is new


Sharing in the sun with you
summer's first tomato,
skin firm yet delicate

He loved another first—
and so I am cast as
the "other-woman type"


"Marry a nice guy, now"
says this guy, with a kiss,
and doesn't marry me


Each having someone waiting,
you and I talk lightly of baseball,
and part in the afternoon


"Here" you say and hand me the ring
"Thanks" I say and take it
like a piece of candy

Evening—
this man who's leaving me
earnestly takes my picture


As I weep, another me
marvels at my weeping—
quietly, love draws to an end


Farewell scene:
do cooling passions
flare up a little at the end?


You and I under the full moon
groping for answers—
like a game of blindman's bluff

Dawn breaks in Tokyo;
at a vending machine in a corner of town,
buying two cans of Coke


As I gaze skyward it floats in my mind—
the name of the girl
who's probably seeing you off


On a hill west of the capital,
where I came once before,
I wave to the Sunshine Building


Holding a daisy high in the air,
both hands around its neck,
I ask "Who do you love best?"

The ancient maiden Sano no Chigami:
to her was granted
the pain of waiting


Slow-motion walk, alone,
through this land that boasts
    the gentle word *natanezuyu*.
rain at rape-blossom time


I boil three chestnuts
to make an autumn for one—
remembering the far-off sea, and you


Voice lowered to a whisper
the pavement fortune-teller confides,
"I see signs of marriage ahead"

Autumn night, wanting a small
    romance—
parsley on the veranda
turning slightly yellow


On the table
I keep a small coconut palm
for my solitary mornings


Won't ease my sighing, I know,
but I try slicing
the ham a bit thicker


Early morning,
cyclamen flowers standing erect—
if only I could see with their eyes

Memories—
like a package of mixed vegetables
that mustn't be defrosted


Unable to follow after someone
leaving on a journey at a whim—
my life goes on as usual


The wonder of it—
a bit of love rests on my palm
after crossing the ocean airmail


Loneliness of being in love
in December—
my heart impervious to "Jingle Bells"

Even dressed up like an antique doll
some of life's mud
cannot be concealed


To pass a day with nothing to do
I play a solitary game:
"pretending to wait for someone"


What sad and weeping voice is that?
Turn and see
steam rising from the rice cooker


Nineteen eighty-five, the year I fell in love,
winds to an end—
in my room, just me and my dieffenbachia

"The crocuses are out"
Suddenly I want to write a letter
opening with those words


Looking at a postcard
from a country of primary colors—
like the sequel to a dream


On the terrace, red with sunrise,
the fern puts out new fronds
to mark the coming of spring


On my table, coffee aroma so rich—
to think of living
with nothing but love!

## Salad Anniversary

Through the falling rain,
a shower of shivering "S" sounds,
I watch your umbrella recede


Your disappearing figure,
a little too cool—
it's always the man
   who sets off on a journey


My profile a year from now—
what will it be looking at,
who will it be looking at?

I remember your hands,
your back, your breath,
your white socks lying
    where you took them off


I long to see the festival in Goa,
but here I am stuck
in this land of Japan


Standing in the subway exit,
it hits me—
there's no one waiting for me


Wait for whom, for what?
The verb "to wait"
was never so intransitive

"One basket 100 yen"
Tomatoes lined up at the shopfront
wear a disgruntled look


Happy in the kitchen
at the sight of broad beans
scattered like musical notes


Folding towels,
I wrap the smell of the sun—
perhaps one day I too shall be a mother


The flow of the river—
whatever I compare it to leaves out
the stones at the bottom

Sucking on a sugar cube
at the wane of spring,
I strip off the T-shirt
    of my twenty-third year

Rugby ball bounds for joy,
concentrating in itself
all the pleasure of the struggle

Giving up on your love
today I try the season's
first linen skirt, first iced coffee

Dream of climbing up and up
a flight of stone stairs—
the steps don't fit my stride

Mysterious creature am I—
though lacking love,
I donate blood


Take off my contacts, blink,
and once again I'm Machi-chan,
alone


Taking my bruised heart,
I hurl it with all my might—
let tomorrow's skies be clear!


Mornings I set back
my fast-running watch
I feel a nameless premonition

Wanting to steep myself
in the time before we meet,
I ride to Shinjuku on the local train


This tale has already begun—
I'm on a moving train
and my ticket says "no stopovers"


Until I see your figure
appear at the station gate
I go on stacking blocks of time


You hurry to me from work,
on your shoulder a golden thread—
a badge of masculinity

Wind at the night game
brushes against your profile
lit the color of grapefruit


Leaving on the platform only
my longing to stay with you,
I board the last train


I study the picture postcard
you sent on your business trip—
like a photo for an alibi


As you take out a handkerchief
a summer butterfly perches
on the plaid of your cotton shirt

"This tastes great," you said and so
the sixth of July—
our salad anniversary


Toast turning golden brown,
and in my room the air
turning slowly into summer


Snapping a shirt smartly
to take out the wrinkles
my heart sparkles white in the sun

# *Twilight Alley*

At the speed of the spreading sunset
croquettes in the back of the
     butcher shop
fry a golden brown

Chinese cabbages with red sashes
side by side at the shopfront
preening and tittering

As if covered all over with
little-girl fingernails
sea bream shine at the fish shop

In the middle of the night
canned green peas
whisper "open up, open up"


Amid the pale blue of small bills
cabbages are laughing—
here in Twilight Alley

# My Bisymmetrical Self

Deciding to return home to live
I close my eyes to a furtive whisper:
"Sad, sad"


Time flows on…
laden with misgivings and regrets,
time flows on its amber way


Caught between two choices
I lie spread-eagled—
in perfect bilateral symmetry

The smell of bread I baked with Mother
on a midsummer afternoon—
put away the memory


The day I left home, Dad muttering
not "So you're off"
but "So you're leaving us"


The day I left for Tokyo
Mother looked older by all the years
of separation ahead


Fukui Station, where I left Mother
with a light "See you, then"—
as if going shopping

In the sun
peace seemed so mundane—
what have I thrown away?


Buy myself a pair of slippers
yellow as spring flowers
now that I live here


Next door, hanging out quilts to air—
rattle of the window opening
echoes with spring


Spitting out the day's fatigue,
    taking it on again,
round and round it goes—
evening train on the Yamanote Loop Line

Beautician who's cut my hair three times
asks me as I take my seat
"Is this your first time here?"


Living alone—
rotten lemon in my right hand
hardly an event


On a night when the world has
    forgotten me
the phone next door rings
on and on


Haven't watered my plants
for three days now—
as if taking some sort of revenge

Long-distance call from Mother—
discuss the prospects
of her herbs and tomatoes


VCR
bought to capture
my five minutes on TV


Your fragrance—
suddenly turn, knowing it can't be you:
summer festival in my hometown


Admonished to stop writing of romance—
what's poetry, then?
Just another way to get a man?

After a muddled conversation, I wonder—
was I expecting too much
of ties with my mother?


Days of wanting to doubt one another—
my mother with sagging breasts,
and her daughter, me


My kid brother, who's never been in love,
takes me to the movies—
I want to look pretty


My favorite singers, the Southern All Stars—
kid brother now old enough
to listen to them too

From the second floor I watch
my mother's umbrella, a glowing red—
like a watercolor by Chihiro Iwasaki


Out in the garden
I pluck a morning tomato—
yes, this is home


Slip out of my T-shirt—
feeling Mother's gaze
trace over me


Making sushi with Mother,
summer comes to an end—
I chew a hempseed, savoring the taste

Hug my kid brother,
lover of chocolate parfaits—
I'm off once more, leaving home again


Persimmons sent from home—
their warm glow brightens
my single room


Before the day is out
    I really must do something—
gourmet mushrooms from Mother,
a bit of a nuisance


Winter brings a chill even to the heart—
as cold winds blow
my phone bill goes up

Warmly recommended by my mother—
this handcream called
"You-skin A"


Back home on an excursion ticket
good for a limited time—
layover in my hometown


At the bus stop I meet a boy
who speaks my native dialect
with perfect courtesy


In my hometown, children's boots
running in the snow
like a sprinkling of bright gumdrops

Ordinary conversations, ordinary smiles—
the ordinariness of home
is what I like best


From mother-and-daughter
we turn into a pair of women—
an age when I think of marrying


Roasting ginkgo nuts—
my thoughts turn to the gentle universe
of home and family


Examining old New Year's cards,
I sort the senders into piles—
this year draws to a close

New Year's Eve—
back in my old home,
complain to Mother my toothbrush is gone


Groping in the mailbox
of my solitary room—
already my face has back its Tokyo feel


January—the soft curve of the daffodil
bending its head
sets me thinking of home

# So, Good Luck

Soccer goalposts
face each other across the field
in a meditative rain


Cherries cherries cherries—
they blossom and disappear,
and the park goes on, unaffected


Pass by two lovers
shyly sharing an umbrella—
ordinary things take on new zest

Passing in the street,
we bow—
hey, that was my corner grocer


Hydrangea:
cast my affections
on the palest purple cluster


Frying onion,
I wait for your call—
until the pungency turns sweet


Bought a new body shampoo—
day turns to night
so that I can shower

Wanting to be loved with abandon,
I run—
June, sandals, hydrangea


Monday morning starts
so that I can see you
Friday at six


After an hour, still no you—
I buy a box of caramels
and wait five minutes more


On Saturday you come to see me,
office man in tennis shoes—
like an unknown creature

An orange blouse
rather than a white one—
it's that sort of romance


Expertly you tuck away a rice-stuffed omelet,
and I make a mental note:
"Likes ketchup"


Another discovery tonight—
watching you push aside asparagus
in your crabmeat salad


You talk of your work
with such a dependable air—
your dependability is what I mainly
    understand

Your occasional Mild Seven Lights—
perhaps in the smoke
you dispel discontent


At a Western-style restaurant
our fried shrimp appear
your tail and mine, neatly aligned


I want to tell you that I love you
but first let me edge a bit farther
from the safety zone


My friend fries cream croquettes—
well, after all
she's a brand-new wife

"Be an ordinary girl"
Listening, I munch
on spicy-hot snacks


Tomatoes ripening
on the supermarket shelf—
sadder than frozen vegetables?


Coffee time for two—
unsettled as a day
when I've forgotten my handkerchief


Station worker's greeting
to homebound passengers at night
strangely comforts my weary heart

Waiting for the train, watching the time
turn from 7:23 (what's it going to be?)
to 7:24 (what it was before…)


"So, good luck…"
writing this last letter
in a corner of McDonald's


Past this hill
the road goes straight to the sea—
I slip through the yellow light

# *Jazz Concert*

The guitarist's mouth,
half open as he plays—
jazz, a downpour of sound and rhythm

The drum beats on, never knowing
of the staves pounding rhythmically
into my flesh

Standing on the amplifier
where horizontal and
    vertical sound waves converge—
a can of beer

By the end of the musicians'
second number
I am drenched in notes


Photographer
snapping away at the stage—
he, too, master of his instrument


Like a hit man
he peers into his camera
wrapped in layers of blue smoky air


On the shoulder of the man
with the silver trumpet,
black shadow of the mike

Concert over,
houselights smile faintly
in the pause before the everyday world
    returns


On the stage, tangled cords lie sprawled
like bars of melted music
fallen off the page


Walking after jazz
through an underground arcade—
hawkers' cries like the rumbling of the sea


Morning—
my inner ear tingles
with the banked fires of last night's jazz

## Backstreet Cat

I smash the eggshell,
crushing "good-bye"
to millimeter units


All day Thursday
I trust the discomfort index—
it's the weather's fault I feel so glum


Lonely—
turn on the TV and see
a woman strangling a man

Red cow
tethered to my keyholder
sometimes shakes its head


Like the morning paper
you slipped into my life
and the word "beginning" took on a glow


The sight of you from behind
reading a paperback as you wait for me—
slightly maddening


I'll pace myself,
write to you only at two-day intervals,
to make it through this season

Watching you
about to tackle
the last strand of spaghetti


Sticking out of my bike basket
somehow they delight me—
celery leaves!


You always bring camera and
    tripod along—
today let's keep it
just the two of us


Say good night to you and think,
now the phone doesn't have to ring
anymore today

Days I missed the forecast,
whether it rains or shines
I don't get mad


The gentleness of sunshine
filtering through purple cosmos
that know nothing of last fall


At that turn on the way to the station
alone, I veer
toward the mailbox


Make a date with you for tomorrow
and slip oh so easily
into the green of sleep

Imagining your pain
at making me wait
I keep on waiting


Along the Sumida River
blows an early winter wind—
grasses tremble nervously


As the boat pulls in loaded with fishermen
you snap the shutter;
I like that look in your eye


Three-thirty p.m. in a noodle shop—
listening to the whisper
of frying tempura

Just now—
thinking of your work, weren't you?
Mumbling only "Eh? Mm."


In a backstreet
my eyes meet the stare of a white cat—
this corner of old Tokyo, a crack in time


Red pepper hotness
of the words I failed to say,
bitter in my mouth


Children come to the candy store
to buy a 10-yen dream—
green bottles of lemon soda

Across the steam you stand
panting and gasping,
gulping down a bowlful of hot *oden* stew


You look great
in your pocket-covered jacket—
shopping in American Alley


Buying lottery tickets
we plan our escape—
spread out a world map balanced
    on an "if"


"Photographer"—
somehow the word
quivers with your gentleness

Your blue sweater
passed in ceremony through
    the station gate,
and disappeared


Looking at a snapshot
too new to be a memory,
I examine my expression


Flipping through the channels,
three times I'm told
"See you next week!"

# Always American

Because it was a spring
full of things to forget,
I listen all day to the Southern All Stars


"Let's go to Spain," you say
as we run down a windy slope—
and I want to go


With your right hand,
where the Line of Fate runs deep,
you slather sauce on your pork cutlet

A girl who likes fortune-telling
keeps trying—
until a lucky card comes up


Sunday—
we're two people in the roadside crowd,
eyes turned on marathon runners


Our coffee, always "American,"
hearts in love think alike—
or cancel each other out


In Hiroshima dialect
you're making fun of our love—
or am I hoping that you are?

Between us the word "good-bye"—
an evening of short questions
and short answers


Memories of being loved,
somehow transparent—
always alone, forever alone

# AFTERWORD

Machi Tawara, a shy, 26-year-old high school teacher living in Tokyo, took Japan by storm with the publication of her maiden work: a book of poetry called *Sarada kinenbi*, here translated as *Salad Anniversary*. In six months the book sailed through countless printings and has sold to date a mind-boggling 2,500,000 copies and more, making it one of the nation's all-time bestsellers. Such a record is remarkable enough for any book, in any genre; for a book of modern poetry it is unprecedented.

"Salad Phenomenon" is the phrase coined to describe the impact of this book on Japanese society. Tawara herself became an instant celebrity, besieged with requests for autographs, interviews, public lectures, guest columns in newspapers and magazines, and TV and radio appearances—all the while keeping up a busy eight-to-five teaching schedule, Mondays through Saturdays. She has had *two* weekly television shows. There have also been a couple of televised serial dramas and a musical revue based loosely on *Salad Anniversary*, not to mention a full-length movie.

Critical reaction has also been highly favorable, despite cavils from purists offended by Tawara's modern adaptation of a classical verse form. "August Morning," the book's opening 50-poem sequence, was awarded the coveted Kadokawa Tanka Prize—an unheard-of achievement for a young woman fresh out of college. The entire book was also named by the Association of Modern Poets as the outstanding poetry collection of 1987.

Besides producing a book of essays and a second slender collection of poems, Tawara came up with a sort of telephone version of the "Prairie Home Companion": touched by the massive outpouring of fan mail she began to receive, and determined somehow to respond, she made short, semi-monthly recordings to chat about her latest doings and announce upcoming events. Meanwhile, the Salad Phenomenon has also brought us comics, choral works by a distinguished composer, and even a CD of "Salad Classics"—Chopin and Debussy—to play while leafing through the book.

Perhaps the most amazing response to Tawara's work has come directly from readers themselves: inspired by Tawara's seemingly effortless sketches of modern life and love, done in an age-old form, many have decided to try their own hand at poetry. Letters have come pouring in by the tens of thousands—and with them, well over 200,000 tanka. Nearly 1,500 of these, selected by Tawara, have also been published in book form. The oldest contributor is a 91-year-old man; the youngest, an 11-year-old girl. One struggles to think of a comparable level of response to any other single work of literature: an identification so complete that readers—people from all walks of life—do not stop at passive enjoyment, but begin a spontaneous creative outpouring of their own.

What is all the fuss about? Tanka (short poems of thirty-one syllables in a 5-7-5-7-7 pattern) have a venerable history of at least 1,300 years in Japan. In modern times, however, they have suffered from an image problem: dealing traditionally with set themes (the beauties of nature, confessions of emotion), tanka tended to become stale and conventional; this difficulty was compounded by poets' continued use of outmoded "literary" language which made the poems hard to understand and kept them seemingly remote from daily experience. Poets who sought to revitalize tanka by avoiding classical formulas, on the other hand, often seemed to achieve modernity at the expense of rhythm and grace. Part of Tawara's achievement lies in her ability to use fresh, contemporary language—skillfully incorporating bits of natural conversation, borrowed words from English like "photographer," and modern icons like McDonald's—without sacrificing the traditional tanka virtues of concision, evocativeness, and musicality.

But Tawara does not limit herself exclusively to the vernacular. She avails herself of a wide range of Japanese, including classical words ("ones I particularly like"). Several *makura-kotoba*, or "pillow words"—traditional poetic modifiers—appear, and there are allusions to individual older poems and to the eighth-century *Man'yoshu*, Japan's oldest poetry anthology. The language employed is thus not mere "young people's Japanese" but a literate, sophisticated mixture of old and new—with emphasis, throughout, on new.

This combination of old and new is present in the opening poem (though impossible, alas, to suggest in translation):

> *Kono kyoku to kimete kaigan zoi no michi*
> *tobasu kimi nari "hoteru kariforunia"*

> Always playing this song
> you race along the seacoast road—
> "Hotel California"

Here the word *nari* is a classical copula, contrasting with the modern, American flavor of the song title.

The same poem illustrates another feature of her work—the tendency for meaning to straddle, not coincide exactly with, the 5-7-5-7-7 syllabic groupings. "Ki-me-te-ka-i-ga-n" (literally, "deciding seacoast") is a 7-syllable cluster in the poem above, but decidedly not a unit of meaning in itself. Tanka are often described as "five-line" poems, but this is misleading in several respects—not least being the fact that they are almost always written in a single line in Japanese. All of the poems in *Salad Anniversary* appear in the original as a single vertical line, three to a page; however, several are interrupted with a space to mark a major break in the poem—a break which may appear at any point. In her second tanka collection, *Toritate no tanka desu* ("Fresh-picked tanka"), Tawara has experimented with writing tanka in two and three lines of various lengths (although she claims that "in her heart" she still thinks of tanka as a single line). In my translations I have generally adhered to a three-line format, and have aimed at brevity without attempting to duplicate syllable counts.

What has so endeared these poems to the Japanese public? One answer seems to be the cheerful, light tone—perfectly suited to the fresh, crisp, "salad" image. The emotions are genuine and deeply felt, but never bitter or overwhelming. The sadness of ending a relationship is balanced by relief, the decision swift and clean:

> Like getting up to leave
>   a hamburger place—
> that's how I'll leave
> that man

She seems to be standing at a slight remove from herself, never totally lost in an emotion, but always partly outside it, observing herself and those around her with a light and coolly objective eye.

Although love, or the lack of it, is the main focus of Tawara's poetry, she writes also of home and family; of life in a big city; of her experiences teaching; of music and cooking and baseball and the sea; of travels in China; of odd moments of sudden insight or whimsy, premonition, or surprise:

> The day I left for Tokyo
> Mother looked older by all the years
> of separation ahead

As in the title poem, she values the ordinary things in life, the small events, finding beauty in them and in a life where every moment is intensely, fully lived:

> "This tastes great," you said and so
> the sixth of July—
> our salad anniversary

> Writing on the blackboard,
>     I pause to rest my hand—
> in those seconds
> think meltingly of you

Ultimately the appeal of her poems rests on their universality, on our recognizing as we read them "Yes, that's just how it is!" or "I know that feeling, too." She says she seeks to express the "swayings of the heart" (*kokoro no yure*); that she succeeds is clear from the reverberations she sets up in our hearts. In her own afterword to her poems she sums up by saying that "to live is to create poetry, to create poetry is to live." It is ironic that (if we may believe her) Machi Tawara has no real lover; these real-sounding love poems spring largely from imagination, based (she says shyly) not on a particular longing for any one person so much as a general longing for human contact. That her poems have moved the hearts of so many, touching the lives of millions of people with whom she would never otherwise have had communication, seems to please her enormously.

*Juliet Winters Carpenter*
*Kyoto, 1989*

## AVAILABLE AND COMING SOON
## FROM PUSHKIN PRESS

Pushkin Press was founded in 1997, and publishes novels, essays, memoirs, children's books—everything from timeless classics to the urgent and contemporary.

Our books represent exciting, high-quality writing from around the world: we publish some of the twentieth century's most widely acclaimed, brilliant authors such as Stefan Zweig, Yasushi Inoue, Teffi, Antal Szerb, Gerard Reve and Elsa Morante, as well as compelling and award-winning contemporary writers, including Dorthe Nors, Edith Pearlman, Perumal Murugan, Ayelet Gundar-Goshen and Chigozie Obioma.

Pushkin Press publishes the world's best stories, to be read and read again. To discover more, visit www.pushkinpress.com.

**THE PASSENGER**
ULRICH ALEXANDER BOSCHWITZ

**TENDER IS THE FLESH**
**NINETEEN CLAWS AND A BLACK BIRD**
AGUSTINA BAZTERRICA

**AT NIGHT ALL BLOOD IS BLACK**
**BEYOND THE DOOR OF NO RETURN**
DAVID DIOP

**WHEN WE CEASE TO UNDERSTAND THE WORLD**
**THE MANIAC**
BENJAMÍN LABATUT

**NO PLACE TO LAY ONE'S HEAD**
FRANÇOISE FRENKEL